A JOURNEY WITH JESUS

Stations of the Cross for School Children

James Allen, O.M.l.

Adapted from *Journey of Decision*
by Sarah A. O'Malley, O.S.B.,
and Robert D. Eimer, O.M.l.

A Liturgical Press Book

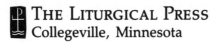 THE LITURGICAL PRESS
Collegeville, Minnesota

To my parents,
Gregory and Cecilia Allen,
who used to take me to
the Stations of the Cross
on Fridays of Lent.

Special Thanks to the principals, teachers, and children of the schools that prayed these Stations of the Cross and told me that they work!

St. Casimir School, St. Paul, Minnesota
St. Thomas the Apostle School, Phoenix, Arizona
St. Teresa School, Belleville, Illinois
Little Flower School, Richmond Heights, Missouri

Cover design by Ann Blattner.
Illustrations by Sr. Mary Charles McGough, O.S.B.

ISBN 13: 978-0-8146-2306-0
ISBN 10: 0-8146-2306-9

SUGGESTIONS FOR USE

The story of the passion and death of Jesus retains all the drama and pathos that it had on the first Good Friday. Children still respond to these events with great understanding and with deep compassion, especially if they can see that the story has meaning for them today. It is to bring children closer to Jesus in the paschal mystery that we have adapted *Journey of Decision.*

We have designed these stations so as to engage the children as much as possible. Fourteen readers represent characters from the passion of Jesus. Giving them some symbolic costume or prop will make the experience more meaningful for them. For example, Pontius Pilate could have a laurel crown; Veronica, her veil; Longinus, his spear; the two criminals, large cardboard crosses; etc.

A student taking the part of Jesus (white robe with red or purple cloak) could carry the processional cross and stand under each station. The readers could stand either in the sanctuary or face the Jesus figure at their assigned station.

The Prayer Leader could be the parish priest, the school principal, the director of religious education, a teacher, a parent, an older student, etc.

The service lasts about 45 minutes.

OPENING PRAYER (ALL):

Loving Jesus, we believe that you carried your cross to Calvary and died there for our sins. As we begin this Way of the Cross with you today, we want to understand what happened on that Good Friday so long ago. Show us how much you loved us. Please be with us in every step of our own journey through life.

3

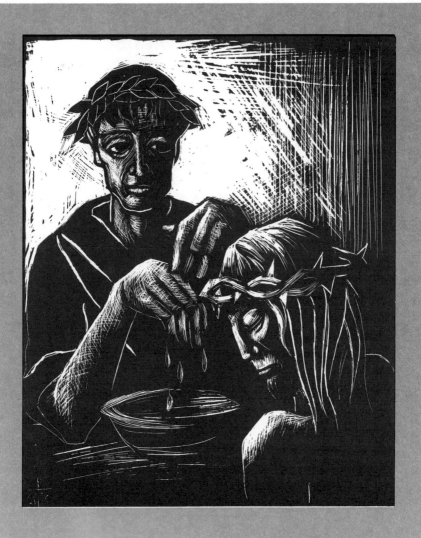

FIRST STATION

PONTIUS PILATE CONDEMNS JESUS TO DIE ON THE CROSS

LEADER: We adore you, O Christ, and we praise you.

ALL: Because by your Holy Cross you have redeemed the world.

READER 1:   **Pontius Pilate**

My name is Pontius Pilate. I am the man that the Roman emperor sent to rule over the Jews in Palestine. They were a hard people to please. Once when I tried to put pictures of the emperor in the temple at Jerusalem, the people got very angry. Then the leaders of the people brought this man Jesus to me. They asked me to kill him on a cross. They even said that he claimed to be the Son of God. I was afraid. I would not dare try to kill a god. I was even more afraid that the Jewish leaders would report to the emperor that I was a traitor. They said to me; "If this man goes free, Pilate, you are no friend of Caesar." Well, I let them have their way with Jesus. What would you have done in my place?

ALL: Jesus, without your help, we are like Pilate. We are afraid and sometimes we do things we should not do. Remind us that, when we hurt those who are innocent, we hurt you too. Give us strength to say "NO" when someone wants us to do things we should not do.

5

SECOND STATION

JESUS HAS TO CARRY HIS OWN CROSS

LEADER: We adore you, O Christ, and we praise you.

ALL: Because by your Holy Cross you have redeemed the world.

READER 2:   **Barabbas, the Rebel**

My name is Barabbas. I was in jail with Jesus because I had tried to kill some Roman soldiers. But Pilate let me go free. It was a big holiday in Jerusalem and the Romans used to let one prisoner go free. Some people wanted Pilate to let Jesus go, but the leaders who hated Jesus got their friends to ask for my freedom. I saw Jesus take up his cross without saying anything. I hated my enemies, but Jesus seemed to love the people who were mean to him. What would you have done?

ALL: Jesus, you told us to forgive our enemies and do good to those who hurt us. That's very hard for me to do. I want to hit and hurt and say mean things to anyone I do not like. But I will try to be like you and show kindness instead. Thank you for showing me the way of love.

THIRD STATION

JESUS FALLS DOWN THE FIRST TIME

LEADER: We adore you, O Christ, and we praise you.

ALL: Because by your Holy Cross you have redeemed the world.

READER 3:   **King Herod of Galilee**

I am King Herod. From my palace window I saw Jesus stumble and fall under the cross. He said once that anyone who wants to be his follower has to take up the cross and follow him. What a strange man he was! Who would ever *want* to suffer? I like to have fun. I would have saved Jesus if he had worked some tricks, some miracles, for me. But he would not even speak to me. I had killed his cousin John the Baptist. Jesus should have been afraid of me. But he just stood there and looked at me.

ALL: Jesus, Herod called you a fool, but I believe in you. Sometimes I find life hard because I want everything to be easy. Help me to learn that, by carrying my own little cross, the hard things of my life, I become more like you.

FOURTH STATION

JESUS MEETS MARY HIS MOTHER

LEADER: We adore you, O Christ, and we praise you.

ALL: Because by your Holy Cross you have redeemed the world.

READER 4:   **Mary, the Mother of Jesus**

Jesus was my little boy. I held him in my arms in a stable at Bethlehem. I watched him grow up. When he was twelve, Joseph and I lost him for many hours. Finally, we found him in the Temple. He told us that he had to be about his Father's business. Is this cross "his father's business"? I felt so sad to see him suffer and bleed, but I believe he knows what he must do for the world. I looked into his eyes and saw only love, love for me and for you. Isn't my son wonderful?

ALL: Jesus, our own mothers love us very much. We know how sad your mother was to see you suffer. Help us always to be loving and kind to our parents, our grandparents, and our teachers. Let us see in them your messengers for us on earth.

FIFTH STATION

SIMON HELPS JESUS CARRY THE CROSS

LEADER: We adore you, O Christ, and we praise you.

ALL: Because by your Holy Cross you have redeemed the world.

READER 5: **Simon of Cyrene**

My name is Simon. I am a farmer from the town of Cyrene. On that Friday morning, I had come up to Jerusalem from the fields where I worked. I saw a big crowd of people, so I went to see what was happening. All of a sudden, a Roman soldier grabbed me and made me carry the cross for a man condemned to die. I was very angry. I had not done anything wrong. But then I saw the man's face. His name was Jesus. He smiled as if to thank me. All of a sudden, the cross seemed lighter. All of a sudden, I was glad to help this poor man carry his cross. After that, I found it easier to help other people who were in trouble.

ALL: Jesus, sometimes I feel lazy. Sometimes I do not like to help other people. But you told us that you want your followers to serve others. Give me a generous and loving heart so that I can do good for everyone.

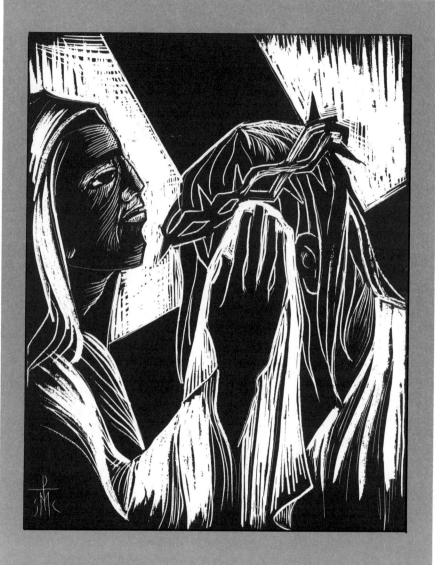

SIXTH STATION

VERONICA WIPES THE FACE OF JESUS

LEADER: We adore you, O Christ, and we praise you.

ALL: Because by your Holy Cross you have redeemed the world.

READER 6:   **Veronica of Jerusalem**

I am Veronica. My home is on the street that leads to the place where the Romans crucified prisoners. I was in my doorway watching Jesus go by. I remember hearing him say, "As long as you give a cup of cool water to the least of your brothers or sisters, you give it to me." I wanted to help him, so I pulled the veil from my head and I bent down to wipe the blood and sweat from his face. The soldier almost hit me, but I did not care. Jesus looked at me with love and that is all the thanks I needed.

ALL: Jesus, sometimes I do not even notice when people need my help. Give me eyes that are always open to see how others need me. Give me hands that are always ready to reach out to help those who suffer.

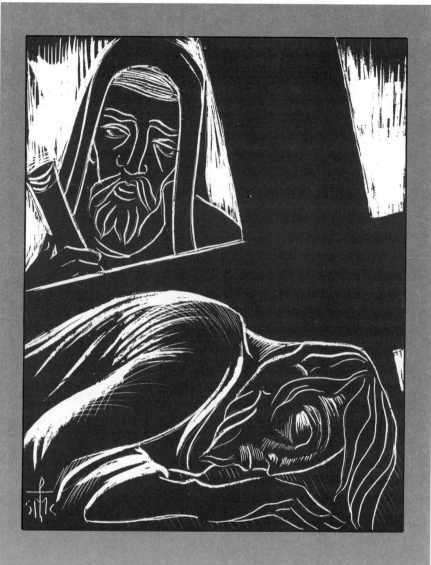

SEVENTH STATION

JESUS FALLS THE SECOND TIME UNDER THE CROSS

LEADER: We adore you, O Christ, and we praise you.

ALL: Because by your Holy Cross you have redeemed the world.

READER 7: **Caiaphas, the High Priest**

My name is Caiaphas, chief priest of the temple in Jerusalem. People came to me and said, "That fellow Jesus is dangerous. He claims to be God. He says he can forgive sins." Who did he think he was? He was just a carpenter from Nazareth. I had to protect my country from the Romans. It was better to get Jesus out of the way than to make the Romans angry with us. So I had him arrested. I saw Jesus fall under his cross, and I laughed to myself. He wouldn't be around much longer, would he?

ALL: Jesus, you loved your country and your people. But some of their leaders did not understand that you were the person God promised to send as their savior. Some of them hated you and planned your death. I want to love my own country. Please make our leaders good and just, at all times to all people.

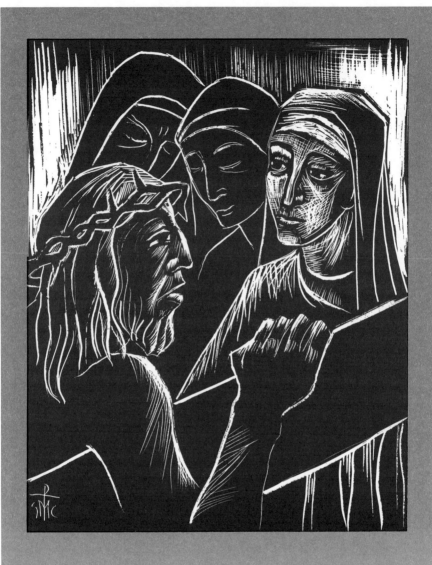

EIGHTH STATION

JESUS MEETS
SOME WOMEN OF JERUSALEM

LEADER: We adore you, O Christ, and we praise you.

ALL: Because by your Holy Cross you have redeemed the world.

READER 8: **A Woman from Jerusalem**

My friends and I had heard Jesus speak a few times. Sometimes we would bake bread and give it to him and his apostles for a snack. Then we saw him bleeding and wearing a crown of thorns. It was just too much. We started to cry. But he stopped and said, "Don't cry for me; rather, cry for yourselves and for your children!" What could that mean? I didn't understand a lot of what he said, but I truly believed he was God's chosen one. Do you believe that too?

ALL: Jesus, many children like ourselves have had to suffer and die in terrible wars. Many children do not have a home to live in nor enough food to eat. We know that you loved children. Help all the mothers and fathers and children of the world.

NINTH STATION

JESUS FALLS THE THIRD TIME
UNDER THE CROSS

LEADER: We adore you, O Christ, and we praise you.

ALL: Because by your Holy Cross you have redeemed the world.

READER 9:   **Longinus, the Roman Soldier**

I'm the Roman soldier who made a crown of thorns and put it on Jesus' head. I'm the one who forced him to get up every time he fell under his cross. But I saw how he forgave the people who hit him and made fun of him. When Jesus was on the cross, I asked him to forgive me for being unkind to him. I believe he truly was the Son of God. I hope you believe that too.

ALL: Jesus, sometimes I fall too, when I sin and do things that go against your love for me. You got up from under your cross. Always pull me up, Jesus, when I fall into sin. Please forgive me, just as you did the Roman soldier.

TENTH STATION

JESUS IS STRIPPED OF HIS CLOTHES

LEADER: We adore you, O Christ, and we praise you.

ALL: Because by your Holy Cross you have redeemed the world.

READER 10:   **The Thief Who Was Not Sorry**

I'm one of the criminals who was crucified with Jesus. I hated the Romans for arresting me and condemning me to die. This Jesus who was on the other cross—they stripped off his clothes and made fun of him, but he didn't even answer back. I don't understand that. To me, he was a wimp. If he was so great, why didn't he free himself and me? All I wanted was to be free. But he did not do it for me. That made me furious. Wouldn't you be angry too?

ALL: Jesus, it must have hurt a lot to be pushed around by the soldiers and made fun of, even by the other criminals. But you showed us how to love and how to forgive. Teach me to be patient with my own hurts and troubles.

ELEVENTH STATION

JESUS IS NAILED TO THE CROSS

LEADER: We adore you, O Christ, and we praise you.

ALL: Because by your Holy Cross you have redeemed the world.

READER 11:   **Dismas, the Thief Who Was Sorry**

My name is Dismas. I used to rob people's homes until they caught me and condemned me to die next to that carpenter from Nazareth. I watched from my own cross as the soldiers nailed Jesus to his. I was surprised to hear him say: "Father, forgive them for they do not know what they are doing." Then I knew he had to be a great man. Then I knew he could help me too. I looked over and asked him to remember me when he came into his kingdom. He smiled through his blood and sweat and said, "Today, you will be with me in paradise." I became a believer. Did you become a believer too?

ALL: Jesus, you promised the thief who was crucified with you that he would be with you in heaven. That is where I want to go when I die too. Help me to forgive those who hurt me. Please forgive me when I hurt others. Make me always ready to be happy with you in heaven.

TWELFTH STATION

JESUS DIES ON THE CROSS

LEADER: We adore you, O Christ, and we praise you.

ALL: Because by your Holy Cross you have redeemed the world.

READER 12:   **Mary Magdalene**

They call me Mary Magdalene. Mine was a difficult and bitter life before I met Jesus. But Jesus looked at me and at so many others with kindness and compassion. He cured our sicknesses and gave us reasons to be happy. He freed me of the evil spirits that had their hold on my life. How then could I stand by and see Jesus hurting and unable to help himself? I so much wanted to help him but all that I could do is stand next to his cross to the very end. I was there when he asked for something to drink. I was there when he cried out: "It is finished." Then he died. My Jesus stopped breathing. I was there to see the death of Jesus. Were you there too?

ALL: Jesus, we could not be there on Calvary hill when you died. But we believe that whenever we go to Mass, you are there in the bread and wine. It's the next best thing to being under the cross. Help us always to know the wonderful story of your Holy Cross.

THIRTEENTH STATION

JESUS' BODY IS
REMOVED FROM THE CROSS

LEADER: We adore you, O Christ, and we praise you.

ALL: Because by your Holy Cross you have redeemed the world.

READER 13: **Salome, the Mother of Two Apostles**

I am Salome, the mother of the apostles James and John. My son James ran away when the soldiers came after Jesus. But John and I didn't run away. We stayed near the cross with Mary, Jesus' mother. I did not understand why Jesus had to suffer. It was only later on that I saw the light. But on that Friday evening, I knew I had to be there to help them take his body off the cross. I had to be there to comfort his poor mother who had lost her only son. Most of Jesus' friends ran away, but Jesus forgave them. Would you have run away?

ALL: Jesus, I do not know if I would have been brave enough to stay with you until the very end. All I know is that from now on, I want to be with you every day of my life. I invite you into my heart and ask you to make my faith stronger than that of your apostles on Good Friday.

FOURTEENTH STATION

JESUS' BODY IS PLACED IN THE TOMB

LEADER: We adore you, O Christ, and we praise you.

ALL: Because by your Holy Cross you have redeemed the world.

READER 14: Nicodemus, the Good Pharisee

I am Nicodemus. I helped my friend Joseph put the body of Jesus in a brand new tomb in a nearby garden. Joseph was braver than I was. He had the courage to ask the Romans for the body. I was always afraid of something. I became a follower of Jesus, but in secret. I came to him only at night so that no one would know I was on his side. After the crucifixion, I was no longer afraid. I was angry and ashamed of myself for not stepping forward earlier to defend Jesus. I helped lay Jesus' body in the tomb. At the time, I did not know it would be there for such a short time.

ALL: Jesus, I believe that you stayed in the tomb only until the following Sunday. Then you rose from the dead. Thank you for dying for me and for coming back to life. You give me a reason to be happy when things do not go so well for me and my family.

LEADER: **Prayers for the Intentions of the Holy Father**

Our Father. . . .
Hail Mary. . . .
Glory be. . . .

31